ISBN:  1732531307
ISBN-13: 978-1732531307

Jimmy- You are my inspiration,
I love you to the moon and back

In Loving Memory of Mia

To all of my family and friends, neighbors, coworkers,
members of the AVM community, nurses and doctors
from Children's Hospital:
Thank you for the support you gave us.
This wouldn't have been possible without you.
XOXO

# My Favorite Star

Written by Lisa Iannucci

Illustrations by Elettra Cudignotto

My sister, Mia, passed away.
It made me very sad.

While I will really miss her,
Mom says heaven isn't bad.

As long as you are good,
the pearly gates you'll meet.

Guaranteed to make you smile,
when you hear that cardinal's tweet.

Once inside, you will see
delightful sights all around.

From rainbow clouds to candy canes,
that come right out of the ground!

Heaven even has a school,
but it isn't your normal day.

You have recess every hour,
so all of your grades are an "A"!

It snows some days,
but it doesn't get too cold.

You can sled on a pancake
over snow made of gold!

Ice cream for dinner?
Sure! Not a big deal.

You don't have to clear your plate
or even finish your meal!

Heaven isn't just for people,
your pets will go there too!

Long as Buster wasn't in too
much trouble,
chewing on dad's new shoe.

There's no TV in heaven,
just too many things to do.

Instead, your angel spends that time
watching over you!

Where is heaven at?
Is it very far?

Just go outside at night
and pick your favorite star.

It sounds so wonderful.
Mom, I want to go!

Not now sweetie pie,
we would miss you more than
you know.

They say things happen for a reason,
though we don't always
understand why.

So let's just focus on the good times,
and know it's still ok to cry.

Mom, will I always be sad
that Mia's not here?

It will get easier with time,
I promise you, my dear.

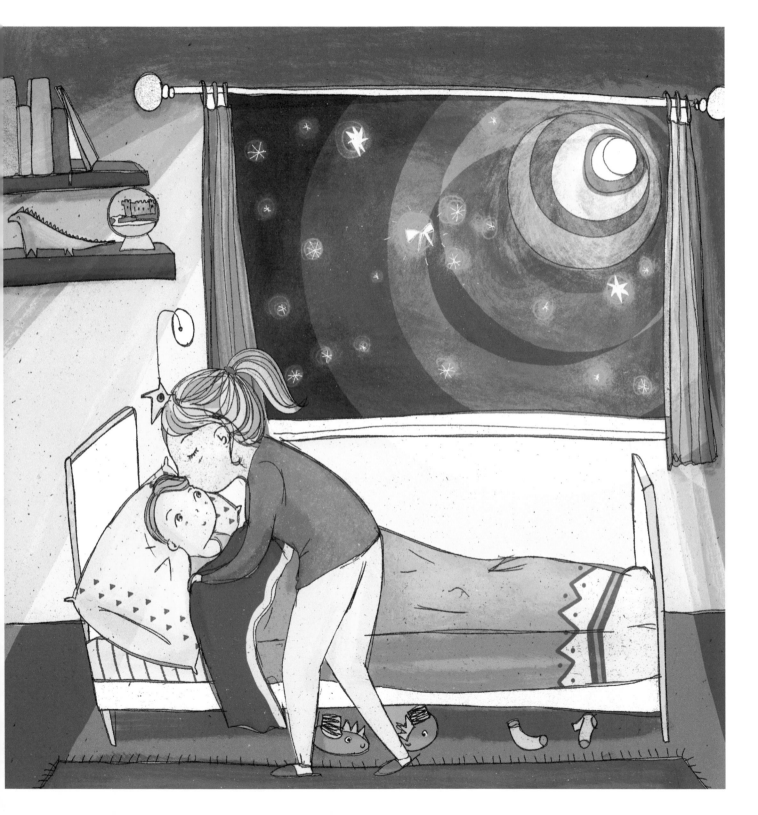

For now when you look
at your star up above,

Know she's watching over
you from heaven, with love.

CPSIA information can be obtained
at www.ICGtesting.com
Printed in the USA
LVHW02n2335171018
593985LV00023BA/458/P